CENGAGE Learning

Drama for Students, Volume 10

Staff

Series Editors: Michael L. LaBlanc.

Contributing Editors: Elizabeth Bellalouna, Anne Marie Hacht, Ira Mark Milne, Jennifer Smith.

Managing Editor: Dwayne Hayes.

Research: Victoria B. Cariappa, *Research Team Manager*. Maureen Eremic, Barb McNeil, Cheryl Warnock, *Research Specialists*. Andy Malonis, *Technical Training Specialist*. Barbara Leevy, Tamara Nott, Tracie A. Richardson, Robert Whaley, *Research Associates*. Scott Floyd, Nicodemus Ford, Sarah Genik, Timothy Lehnerer, *Research Assistants*.

Permissions: Maria Franklin, *Permissions Manager*. Margaret A. Chamberlain, Edna Hedblad, *Permissions Specialists*. Erin Bealmear, Shalice Shah-Caldwell, Sarah Tomasek, *Permissions*

Associates. Debra Freitas, Julie Juengling, Mark Plaza, *Permissions Assistants.*

Manufacturing: Mary Beth Trimper, *Manager, Composition and Electronic Prepress.* Evi Seoud, *Assistant Manager, Composition Purchasing and Electronic Prepress.* Stacy Melson, *Buyer.*

Imaging and Multimedia Content Team: Randy Bassett, *Image Database Supervisor.* Robert Duncan, Dan Newell, *Imaging Specialists.* Pamela A. Reed, *Imaging Coordinator.* Dean Dauphinais, Robyn V. Young, *Senior Image Editors.* Kelly A. Quin, *Image Editor.*

Product Design Team: Kenn Zorn, *Product Design Manager.* Pamela A. E. Galbreath, *Senior Art Director.* Michael Logusz, *Graphic Artist.*

Copyright Notice

Since this page cannot legibly accommodate all copyright notices, the acknowledgments constitute an extension of the copyright notice.

While every effort has been made to secure permission to reprint material and to ensure the reliability of the information presented in this publication, the Gale Group neither guarantees the accuracy of the data contained herein nor assumes any responsibility for errors, omissions, or discrepancies. Gale accepts no payment for listing; and inclusion in the publication of any organization, agency, institution, publication, service, or individual does not imply endorsement of the editors or publisher. Errors brought to the attention of the publisher and verified to the satisfaction of the publisher will be corrected in future editions.

This publication is a creative work fully protected by all applicable copyright laws, as well as by misappropriation, trade secret, unfair competition, and other applicable laws. The authors and editors of this work have added value to the underlying factual material herein through one or more of the following: unique and original selection, coordination, expression, arrangement, and classification of information. All rights to this publication will be vigorously defended.

© 2001 Gale Group, Inc.
27500 Drake Rd.
Farmington Hills, MI 48331–3535

Gale Group and Design is a trademark used herein under license.

All rights reserved including the right of reproduction in whole or in part in any form.

This book is printed on acid-free paper that meets the minimum requirements of American National Standard for Information Sciences—Permanence Paper for Printed Library Materials, ANSI Z39.48-1984.

ISBN 0-7876-4084-0
ISSN 1094-9232

Printed in Canada
10 9 8 7 6 5 4 3 2 1

Lysistrata

Aristophanes 411 B.C.

Introduction

Lysistrata is often produced in contemporary theatre. Modern audiences enjoy the sexuality and humor in Aristophanes' work, and they enjoy what appears as modern feminism and the depiction of strong women. Comedies were very popular presentations during the Greek festivals, and there is no reason to think that *Lysistrata* was not immensely popular. At the time of the play's initial production, Athens and Sparta had been at war for twenty years, and this play would have offered one of the few opportunities to laugh at war. The idea that Lysistrata could unite women to end the war would have set up the audience for a traditional battle between the sexes. However, there are also serious ideas to be found in Lysistrata's speeches. She reminds the audiences of the many men who have died during the Peloponnesian War, and the Chorus of Old Men emphasizes that there are no young men to take up their position. Aristophanes uses a woman to bring peace, but in doing so, he is pointing out to men that they have failed in their efforts to settle the war. With the failure of men, women are the only remaining hope for peace. There is no record that Aristophanes received any awards for *Lysistrata,* but the play's popularity in modern productions points to its probable success on stage. In 1930, *Lysistrata* enjoyed a successful revival in New York City, which lasted for several months. It has inspired an opera, *Lysistrata and the War,* which was written in the early 1960s and first performed by the Wayne State University opera workshop, as a protest to the Vietnam War. The theme of war and women's efforts to invoke love as a replacement for war works as well in the twenty first century as they did in the late fifth century B.C.

Author Biography

Little is known of Aristophanes, except that his father, who was from Athens, may have been a property owner. When Aristophanes was born, Athens was at its most glorious, both culturally and politically. Born at about 450 B.C., Aristophanes was a young man when the Peloponnesian war was fought between Athens and Sparta. This war (431-401 B.C.) provided some of the historical framework for Aristophanes' comedies. Athen's loss in this war affected Aristophanes, and in response, he used comedy to ridicule the political order responsible for the war and the city's loss. Aristophanes' sympathy with the aristocratic landowners and condemnation of the rulers of Athens makes him appear more revolutionary than many of his cohorts. Aristophanes is associated with the Old Comedy, or *comoedia prisca,* which is earthy and irreverent and willing to attack prominent people.

Aristophanes' comedies are the only ones to have survived from this period. Of the forty-four comedies he wrote, eleven have survived. The Athenian festival of Dionysis was the first festival, in 486 B.C., to officially include comedy. Aristophanes entered the festival and won three first prizes, which was less than either of his rivals, Cratinus and Eupolis. The themes of Aristophanes' eleven surviving comedies reflect the poet's dissatisfaction with the government of Athens.

Aristophanes wrote many of his plays during the war between Athens and Sparta. The works that have survived include *Acharnians,* 425 B.C.; *Knight,* 424 B.C.; *Clouds,* 423 B.C. (revised c. 418 B.C.); and *Wasps, All* B.C. Other surviving plays include *Peace, All* B.C.; *Birds,* 414 B.C.; *Lysistrata,* 411 B.C.; *Thesmophoriazusae (Women Keeping the Festival of the Thesmophoriae),* 411 B.C.; and *Frogs,* 405 B.C. The remainder of Aristophanes' extant work includes *Ecclesiazusae (Assemblywomen* or *Women in Parliament)*, 392 B.C.; and *Plutus (Wealth),* 388 B.C. A number of other plays have been lost. Three of these comedies —*Lysistrata, Thesmophoriazusae,* and *Ecclesiazusae*—depict women as the moving force in human society. After his death, Aristophanes' popularity ceased, and he was not rediscovered until the Renaissance, and it was not until modern times that Aristophanes reentered the Western literary canon. In the Byzantine world, however, Aristophanes always held the rank of a major author: he was assiduously copied, studied, and appreciated by scholars.

Plot Summary

The play opens with Lysistrata pacing back and forth as she waits for the other women to arrive. She is impatient and tells her neighbor, Calonice, that women have a reputation for sly trickery, but when they are needed for something important, they lie in bed instead of rushing to meet. Lysistrata tells her neighbor that the safety of all of Greece lies with the actions of the women of Greece. Soon, all the women arrive, and Lysistrata tells them of her plan to end the war between Athens and Sparta. But first the group enters into some ribald joking about their figures and about sex. Lysistrata asks the women if they would not rather their husbands were home instead of fighting elsewhere. When the women reply in the affirmative, Lysistrata relates a plan to have all the women deny their husbands and lovers their sexual favors until the men vow to stop fighting and end the war. The women are difficult to convince, but eventually they agree to the plan. Lysistrata also tells the women that if they are beaten, they may give in, since sex that results from violence will not please the men. Finally, all the women join Lysistrata in taking an oath to withhold sex from their mates.

With Lampito returning to Sparta to secure the agreement of the Spartan women, Lysistrata and the women who remain with her make plans to join the women who have seized the Acropolis and its treasury. Within moments, a group of old men arrive, planning to set the base of the Acropolis on fire and force the women out. The old men complain that the women they have nourished all these years have turned against them and seized a sacred shrine. But while the men are busy with their smoking logs, the women enter, carrying pitchers of water, which they will pour over the fires that the men have set. The old men and old women trade insults, but the women will not back down, and they empty their water over the heads of the old men. When the magistrate arrives, he tells the men that the women's behavior is the result of the men spoiling their women, treating them with gentleness when they do not deserve to be cherished. The magistrate orders that the men force open the doors, but he moves to a safe distance to watch.

When the doors are forced open, Lysistrata emerges. The magistrate orders her arrested, but the policeman is too intimidated by Lysistrata to arrest her. The other women join Lysistrata in defying the policemen, who are too cowed to follow the magistrate's orders to seize the women. The magistrate responds to the women's actions with a claim that they shall never lose to women, and the newly brave police attack the women, but they are soon beaten off and in retreat. When there is calm again, Lysistrata explains that the women have seized the Acropolis to keep men from using the money to make war and to keep dishonest officials from stealing the money. The women say they can administer the money, since they are used to administering the household money. Lysistrata also tells the magistrate that the women have been patient while the men mucked up the war and refused to listen to any advice, but now, the women have decided to take action, since there are few men left in Greece. When the magistrate continues to protest, the women dress him in women's clothing, and then they explain that they will approach the problems of state in the same way that they approach the carding of wool. When the magistrate continues to insult the women, the women dress him as a corpse, and the man runs away. Left to continue the argument, the old men and old women turn to insults again. The old women meet each of the men's insults with rebuttals of their own. They remind the men that women bear children, but men make no contribution. The shouting and insults eventually turns to physical fighting, as both sides strip off their tunics and set upon each other.

Although there is no division of scene, it is understood that an interval of five days has passed since the previous action, and Lysistrata is now dealing with a possible mutiny. Many of the women are deserting and going to the men. Lysistrata tries to convince the women that the men are also miserable sleeping alone, and she pulls out an oracle from the gods telling the women they will win. The women are convinced, and the rebellion is soon ended, as they return to the Acropolis. A group of old men and old women soon enter singing, and Lysistrata calls their attention to a man, who is approaching. Cinesias is mad with passion, and in great pain and distress, since he misses his wife, Myrrhine. But she refuses to abandon her oath and join him, until the men stop the war. Through a succession of maneuvers, Myrrhine teases Cinesias until he is exasperated, and then she leaves him and returns inside. The chorus of old men sympathize with Cinesias, but it is not sympathy that he wants; he is now quite angry. Within moments a magistrate from Athens arrives and is joined by a herald from Sparta. Both are suffering from the women's absence, as are men everywhere. The two agree that something must be done, and the herald returns to Sparta with instructions to return with someone who can arrange a truce. While everyone awaits the peace envoy, the women seek to soothe the men. When the ambassadors arrive, Lysistrata is sent for, and the negotiations begin. But when it appears that neither group can reach an agreement, the men are invited inside to feast. The men's desire for their wives increases with the wine, and soon the treaty is signed, and both men and women leave for their homes.

Characters

Calonice

Calonice (also called Cleonice) is a friend of Lysistrata, but she is at first reluctant to make the sacrifices that Lysistrata asks. Calonice is earthy and funny, especially in voicing her lust for her husband. She becomes one of Lysistrata's strongest supporters, but not without having first been browbeaten by Lysistrata.

Child

Cinesias brings his infant son to the siege in an attempt to convince Myrrhine to return home.

Chorus of Old Men

The chorus of old men leads an assault on the Acropolis. They try to burn the women out by setting fire to the base of the building. When action fails them, the old men engage in a war of words with the old women, who have seized the treasury. The old men are offended by the women's desire to control the treasury, but they are ineffective against the strength of the women.

Chorus of Old Women

The old women prove a formidable force, easily defending the Acropolis against the old men's attack. They pour water on the men, when they attempt to set a fire, and they prove themselves wittier and more effective in a war of words with the old men. The old women point out that men only pass useless laws that lead to disorder.

Cinesias

Cinesias is Myrrhine's husband. He suffers from unfulfilled lust and begs his wife to forget her oath and return to his bed.

Cleonice

See Calonice

Lampito

Lampito is a Spartan woman who agrees with Lysistrata and who helps to bring about peace between the two enemies. She is athletic and bold, and demonstrates that she is also loyal and resourceful. Lampito provides the Spartan equivalent to the Athenian Lysistrata.

Lysistrata

Lysistrata is an idealistic young woman who wants to bring a stop to the war. She decides that the most effective way to get the men to stop fighting is to deny them sex. She brings all the other women together and with some help from Lampito, convinces all the women to join in her in this plan. Lysistrata is smart and funny, a heroine with good analytical abilities, who is easy to admire. She helps the old women defend the Acropolis, thus controlling the treasury and preventing any more money being spent on war. When it appears that many of the women cannot hold out any longer, Lysistrata finds a prophecy that convinces the women to stick with the plan. She displays intelligence and the ability to be creative and convincing. When it appears that the peace talks between Athens and Sparta will end without an agreement, Lysistrata devises additional means to convince the men to find a peaceful solution.

Media Adaptations

- There are no filmed adaptations of this play. However, *Lysistrata,* was adapted as an opera in 1963-1967, to be performed by the Wayne State University opera workshop. There is a 90-minute cassette of the music available from Greenwich Publishers in Saskatchewan, Canada.

Magistrate

The magistrate attempts to convince the women to return home, threatening them with silly and demeaning punishments. His attempts to disband the women fail, and his effectual control over the women illustrates how Aristophanes views the ineffectual government. This character is the target of Aristophanes' ridicule of the governing system and represents the foolishness of the leaders.

Myrrhine

Myrrhine is one of Lysistrata's strongest supporters and a willing captain in her service. When her husband tries to convince her to leave, Myrrhine denies him sexual favors and teases her husband with what he is missing. Her support of Lysistrata's scheme shifts the balance of power and marks the beginning of the men's defeat.

Spartan Envoys

It is the Spartan envoys who finally agree to a

peace.

Spartan Herald

The Spartan herald is one of the men suffering without a woman.

Themes

Obedience

One of the most "shocking" aspects of the women's actions is their disobedience to men. When the men arrive with logs and the intention of burning out the women, they tell the audience that they are shocked that the women they have nourished, and through implication spoiled, have turned on the men. In short, the women of Athens are no longer obedient to the men of Athens. Moreover, the women are willing to trade insults and even to fight, if necessary. This behavior contradicts the expected demeanor of the women. The magistrate, who represents the legal and conventional expectations of women, finds that he has no control. The women first dress him in women's garb and then in the clothing of a corpse. The women have abandoned their traditional roles as obedient wives and daughters, and assumed a position of power.

Sex

It is sex that permits the women to seize control. The men are held captive to their carnal desires and are unable to deal with the women as they had previously. Sex is both the women's weapon and their prize to withhold. Sex gives the women a power they would not ordinarily hold; and with the simple banding together of the women, the desire for sex leads the men to capitulate. One of the women, Myrrhine, uses her sexuality to tease her husband, and to assert her power over him. Near the end of the play, as Lysistrata tries to negotiate a peace, she uses sex to motivate the men, by parading a nude representation of reconciliation in front of the sex-deprived males. When this maneuver fails to work, Lysistrata plies the men with wine, in a ironic reversal of the traditional male effort to seduce a woman. When the men begin drinking they become even more desperate for sex, and finally agree to a truce.

Strength and Weakness

Lysistrata correctly identifies the men's weakness and uses their weakness to create a truce. The women in this play are depicted as strong and brave. They willingly stand up to the old men and to the magistrate. They refuse to be intimidated or frightened from their oath. Instead, the women readily defend their choice and the Acropolis. They understand that a war cannot be fought without money, and that if for some reason the oath to withhold sex fails to work, they will have another tool with which to bargain. Where sex proves to be the women's strength, it is also the men's weakness, since they will promise anything to have sex.

War and Peace

It is war that has devastated Athens. The

chorus is made up of old men because there are no young men left. Those who have not been killed in the war, now in its twentieth year, are off at war. The women remain behind and must manage children and property with little assistance. Young women have no one to wed. Lysistrata says that when men return from war, even the old ones can find wives. But once their time has passed, young women will never find a husband. This is one of the injustices of war, the abandonment of the women. The Peloponnesian War provides the background for this comedy, but the subject, the tragedy that this war brought to Athens, illustrates that war victimizes everyone.

Style

Audience

The people for whom a drama is performed. Authors usually write with an audience in mind. Aristophanes writes for an audience interested in drama as entertainment, but this is also an audience that would expect the playwright to include important lessons about life. In this case, the lesson is about an effective society and government that allows a war to continue after so many years. This comedy uses satire and humor to suggest to the audience that the men in power have not been effective in dealing with the war.

Character

A person in a dramatic work. The actions of each character are what constitute the story. Character can also include the idea of a particular individual's morality. Characters can range from simple stereotypical figures to more complex multifaceted ones. Characters may also be defined by personality traits, such as the rogue or the damsel in distress. *Characterization* is the process of creating a lifelike person from an author's imagination. To accomplish this the author provides the character with personality traits that help define who he will be and how he will behave in a given situation. As is usually the case in Greek drama, the character's names in *Lysistrata* suggest their function. Lysistrata's name means "she who disbands the army."

Chorus

In ancient Greek drama, a chorus consisted of a group of actors who interpreted and commented on the play's action and themes, most often singing or chanting their lines. Initially the chorus had an important role in drama, as it does in *Lysistrata,* but over time its purpose was diminished, and as a result, the chorus became little more than commentary between acts. Modern theatre rarely uses a chorus.

Drama

A drama is often defined as any work designed to be presented on the stage. It consists of a story, of actors portraying characters, and of action. Historically, drama has consisted of tragedy, comedy, religious pageant, and spectacle. In modern usage, drama explores serious topics and themes but does not achieve the same level as tragedy. *Lysistrata is* traditional Greek drama. Just as drama educates and warns, comedy can provide important lessons for men about how they govern. The laughter of the audience makes comedy a safer forum for criticism of the governing body.

Genre

Genres are a way of categorizing literature. Genre is a French term that means "kind" or "type." Genre can refer to both the category of literature such as tragedy, comedy, epic, poetry, or pastoral. It can also include modern forms of literature such as drama novels, or short stories. This term can also refer to types of literature such as mystery, science fiction, comedy, or romance. *Lysistrata* is a Greek comedy, in this case an Old Comedy, which refers to earthy and humorous sexuality.

Topics for Further Study

- How does the comedy in Lysistrata differ from the comedy of one of William Shakespeare's comedies, such as *Taming of the Shrew?*
- Consider the ways in which *Lysistrata* attacks Athenian society and discuss the effectiveness of ridicule and irony in changing

political decisions. Would such satire be effective in attacking politicians today? Or do modern politicians simply ignore satire?

- How are the men's attitudes toward women depicted in this play, and how do the women respond to the men's attack? Who do you think demonstrates the stronger position?

- Research the war between Sparta and Athens. Does Aristophanes' attack on Athenian society reflect the uselessness of this war? That is, is the playwright correct in having Lysistrata point out that both Sparta and Athens would be better off uniting to fight a common enemy?

Farce

Much of the action and most of the dialogue in this play is farcical, filled with nonsense and exaggeration. The action of the play is suppose to be divided over a period of five days, with the women organizing and seizing the Acropolis, and the meeting between Athenian and Spartan ambassadors occurring five days later. Periods of time are never exactly noted, but the time lapse is certainly not long enough to account for the state of misery that the men portray. The emphasis in the play is on their physical discomfort and the obvious signs of that discomfort. The humor is ribald and lewd, with risqué references to just what it is that the women are denying the men.

Plot

This term refers to the pattern of events. Generally plots have a beginning, a middle, and a conclusion, but they may also sometimes be a series of episodes connected together. Basically, the plot provides the author with the means to explore primary themes. Students are often confused between the two terms; but themes explore ideas, and plots simply relate what happens in a very obvious manner. Thus the plot of *Lysistrata* is how women decide to withhold sex to force the men to stop the war. But the theme is how ineffective men have been in bringing an end to a war that has lasted twenty years and which will last another seven years.

Scene

Traditionally, a scene is a subdivision of an act and consists of continuous action of a time and place. However, Aristophanes is not using acts, and so the action, is contained in one scene, covering an unspecified period of time, perhaps a few days at most.

Setting

The time, place, and culture in which the

action of the play takes place is called the setting. The elements of setting may include geographic location, physical or mental environments, prevailing cultural attitudes, or the historical time in which the action takes place. The primary location for *Lysistrata* is Athens. The action spans a space of several days; five days is suggested in the text.

Historical Context

The Peloponnesian War was in its twentieth year when Aristophanes wrote *Lysistrata*. Athens and Sparta had been long-standing enemies, but they had finally negotiated an uneasy peace in 445 B.C. When Athens wanted to extend its empire, the uneasy peace was broken, and war erupted. When the war began in 431 B.C., Greece was not a country as we know it today. Instead it was a collection of small, rival city-states, located both on the mainland and on the surrounding islands. The war began after Sparta demanded certain concessions of Athens, and the Athenian leader Pericles convinced the Athenians to refuse, and instead, go to war. There was a short truce after ten years of fighting, when it appeared that the war was deadlocked between the two city-states; but soon the war resumed. Initially Athens seemed to be winning; in spite of having lost many people to the plague, they were winning some battles and appeared to be stronger than their enemy, Sparta. Sparta even suggested peace, which Athens rejected. But soon, the war changed, with Sparta in the stronger position. Athens had a stronger navy than Sparta, and the Athenian forces commanded the seas, but when the battle shifted, Sparta emerged as the stronger force. A major shift in the war occurred when Athens attempted to invade Sicily. This unsuccessful attack led to serious losses at land and at sea. These losses made Athens more vulnerable to Sparta's land forces, which had always been stronger than those of Athens. In addition, Athens' navy, which had always been its strongest force, had been destroyed in the ill-fated invasion of Sicily. Although Athens' navy was later rebuilt, it was eventually destroyed again by Sparta. By 405 B.C., the war was over and Athens had lost, having suffered near ruin. When Lysistrata reminds the audience of the terrible losses that the city has endured, everyone in the audience would have recognized the truth of her words. The chorus in *Lysistrata* is made up of old men because there are no young men remaining. Lysistrata laments the shortage of men because there are no grooms for the young women who seek husbands. The war, which has lasted twenty long years, shows no sign of ending, when Aristophanes is staging his play. The war will end in another seven years, but only after the Athenians are starved into surrendering.

The end of the war was a major defeat for Athens, one from which it could not recover. A peace agreement was signed in 404 B.C., and Sparta imposed severe penalties on Athens. In addition to surrendering almost all of their remaining ships, Athens was also forced to tear down the city walls, and adhere to the same foreign policy as Sparta. The Peloponnesian War was a catastrophe for Athens, leading to the destruction of her empire. The city continued to exist as a center for culture and wealth, but its political strength was never the same. The city treasury, which Lysistrata and the old women hoped to preserve, was laid waste by a war that lasted twenty-seven years. The government of

Athens changed, as well. There were many political murders, most at the hands of the committee of thirty that Sparta placed in control of Athens' government.

Compare & Contrast

- **c. 411 B.C.:** The democracy of Athens is overthrown by extremists, who are in open negotiation with Sparta. These extremists are soon overthrown, and the Athenian navy defeats the Spartan navy a few months later.

    Today: Greece is a united country at this time, with no city-state attempting to seize control over the country.

- **c. 411 B.C.:** The war between Sparta and Athens has continued for twenty years. The Peloponnesian War will end in 404 B.C., with Athens' defeat.

    Today: Greece, which has been dominated by military coups and turmoil with neighboring Turkey since the end of World War II, is no longer considered a dominant military force.

- **c. 411 B.C.:** In 429 B.C., a plague killed one third, and perhaps as many as two thirds of the population of Athens. Because of this plague, many Athenians ceased to believe in their gods, and much of the population fell into drunkenness, gluttony, and licentiousness. The effect of this change can be seen in the drama, *Lysistrata,* in which there is little mention of the gods-as there had been in many earlier Greek dramas.

Today: Medicine has helped to identify the cause of disease, and most modern populations no longer blame the gods for the plague. But occasionally, as was the case with the initial discovery of AIDS, a segment of the population will attribute the victims' disease to a punishment of god and a judgment on behavior.

- **c. 411 B.C.:** The annual drama prizes at the Dionysus competition continue to draw the most talented dramatists. The prizes are sought after, and even in the midst of war, the leading dramatists of the period continue to challenge one another for prizes and recognition as the greatest playwright.

  Today: Drama competition continues with prizes for film and theatre eagerly sought each spring. Winners of the Best Film at the Academy Awards or the Best Play at the Critic Circle Awards are assured of accolades and monetary rewards that will ease the production of subsequent work.

- **c. 411 B.C.:** 25-35 percent of the population of Greece are slaves, many of whom work in the silver mines.

  Today: Slavery has long since ended, but Greece is now dealing with severe poverty and a shrinking economic base.

Critical Overview

By 411 B.C., the Peloponnesian War had lasted twenty years, and Athens was in a state of turmoil. The plague of a few years earlier had decimated the population, killing anywhere from one-third to two-thirds of the people. At the time of the initial presentation of Aristophanes' *Lysistrata,* probably in January of 411 B.C., the political atmosphere of Athens was one of unrest. Within months, extremists would overthrow the democracy of Athens, and engage in open negotiations with Sparta. Although these extremists would soon be overthrown, their initial success indicates how unstable the atmosphere of Athens was at the time. But those events were still six months away at the time of Aristophanes' play, and there were other events that revealed how difficult life had become for Athenians. Athens had only recently suffered a significant and disastrous military loss in the attempted invasion of Sicily. With the destruction of their navy, the importation of food became a pressing concern for Athens, and serious food shortages and hunger were the result. Although there are many comedic moments in *Lysistrata,* there are many serious moments, such as when Lysistrata tells the magistrate that many of Athens' young men had died, and so, many of the city's young women will never have the chance to marry and have families. Lysistrata's actions will end the war, something that men had not been able to do in the past twenty years. Aristophanes gives important lines to his heroine, a woman, to point out to the audience just how inept their government had become. The Greek audience knew of women's weaknesses, but Lysistrata's strengths illustrate that one weak women can accomplish what men cannot. In Aristophanes' play, women are strong, and they are a force that can end a war.

Since there are no records of how this play was received, and since Aristophanes won no prize for its writing, it is difficult to reconstruct how the audience reacted to this depiction of women as heroic. However, it is possible to examine how well *Lysistrata* has endured by focusing on the play as source material for modern productions. It should not be surprising, given its antiwar motif and the depiction of women as strong movers of social change, that Lysistrata's story has continued to be a popular play in modern productions. Although *Lysistrata* was originally produced as musical comedy, most modern productions either eliminate the music or severely reduce its presence. Although there have been many productions of Aristophanes' play during the past one hundred years, there are two New York productions that offer contrasting views of this play's applicability to modern life. In 1930, *Lysistrata* enjoyed a successful and commercially profitable run on the New York stage. In an evaluation of the reviews from the period, critic Clive Barnes quotes 1930 reviews as pronouncing the play "a smash." Some of these earlier Broadway critics noted that this Greek comedy contained set designs that offered a "rich-hued, towering Acropolis," and that the actors helped to make the play "a delectable desert for Broadway palates." Subsequent productions have not fared so well, with a 1959 Broadway production earning mostly negative reviews. Among the reviewers, none were enthusiastic, but most simply found this new production of *Lysistrata* either dated or offensive. Robert Coleman described the play as "a bit shopworn," while John McClain labeled the play, "tasteless and revolting." Much of McClain's ire was directed toward an attempt to modernize the play through revealing costumes and an emphasis on eroticism.

Aristophanes' audience was committed to the theatre, which was not a daily or even weekly occurrence. The festivals during which the plays were presented demanded something more from an audience than that which modern audiences are prepared to give. Since plays were only presented during the festivals, perhaps a couple of times in a year, Greek audiences arrived early and stayed late. Audiences sat on stone benches from sunrise to sunset, and in the large theatre at Dionysus, seventeen thousand, mostly men, sat to listen to the words of Sophocles, Aristophanes, Euripides, Aeschylus, and others. It would be difficult for today's audience to grasp the excitement that greeted *Lysistrata* when it first appeared on stage, and this is made more difficult in an atmosphere where theatre is readily available every day.

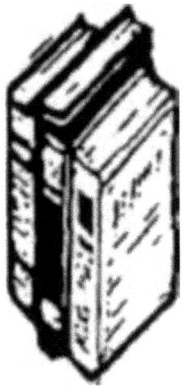

What Do I Read Next?

- *Thesmophoriazusae,* also by Aristophanes, was produced in 411 B.C. Like *Lysistrata,* this play also depicts women as an important force in society.

- *Peace,* also by Aristophanes (421 B.C.), addresses the problem of war, with a stronger presence by the gods of Mt. Olympus.

- *Four Plays by Aristophanes: The Clouds, The Birds, Lysistrata, The Frogs,* is a compilation of four of Aristophanes' plays. This New American Library paperback (1984) is an easy and inexpensive way to become acquainted with this author.

- The Penn Greek Drama Series, *Aristophanes, 2: Wasps, Lysistrata,*

Frogs, The Sexual Congress, (1999) provides a scholarly translation of four of Aristophanes' plays.

- William Shakespeare's, *The Taming of the Shrew* (1592), offers a romantic examination at the war between men and women.
- Menander, a later Greek playwright, also wrote comedy, including, *Samia* (c. 300 B.C.), a romantic comedy about confused identities. Menander represents the new Comedy, but only fragments of his plays are available.

Sources

Aristophanes, *Lysistrata,* edited by Jeffrey Henderson, The Focus Classical Library, 1992.

Arkins, Brian, "Sexuality in Fifth-Century Athens," in *Classics Ireland,* University College, 1994.

Barnes, Clive, compilation of reviews of the 1930 production of *Lysistrata,* in *New York Times Directory of the Theatre,* Arno Press, 1973.

Coleman, Robert, review of *Lysistrata,* in *Daily Mirror,* November 25, 1959.

McCain, John, review of *Lysistrata,* in *Journal American,* November, 15, 1959.

Motto, Anna Lydia, and John R. Clark, "Lysistrata: Overview," in *Reference Guide to World Literature,* 2nd ed., edited by Lesley Henderson, St. James Press, 1995.

Tyrrell, William Blake, and Larry J. Bennett, "Pericles' Muting of Women's Voices in Thuc. 2.45.2," paper delivered at the Kentucky Foreign Language Conference, 1999.

Woolf, Virginia, "A Room of One's Own: Shakespeare's Sister," in *The Lexington Reader,* D.C. Heath & Co., 1987, pp. 50-60, originally published in 1929.

Further Reading

Bowie, A. M., *Aristophanes: Myth, Ritual, and Comedy,* Cambridge University Press, 1996.

> This book uses the techniques of cultural anthropology to compare Aristophanes' plays with Greek myths and rituals. This book also attempts to reconstruct the probable reaction of the audience to these plays.

MacDowell, Douglas M., *Aristophanes and Athens: An Introduction to the Plays,* Oxford University Press, 1995.

> This book provides information about the political background of Aristophanes' plays and is very helpful to new readers or audiences, who might lack an understanding of the political and social forces behind this writer's work.

Rehm, Rush, *Greek Tragic Theatre,* Routledge, 1994.

> This book is helpful to readers who want to understand how Greek tragedy works. This author looks at performances of several plays and encourages readers to consider the context in which the plays were

performed.

Strauss, Barry S., *Fathers and Sons in Athens: Ideology and Society in the Era of the Peloponnesian War,* Princeton University Press, 1993.

> This text examines how social upheaval, especially during time of war, affects the family, especially the relationship between father and son. Strauss also draws connections between the problems that faced Athenian families and the dynamics of modern families.

Thucydides, *History of the Peloponnesian War,* Penguin Classics, 1986.

> Thucydides' great history of the war between Sparta and Athens remains one of the great histories of all time.

Walton, J. Michael, *Living Greek Theatre,* Greenwood, 1987.

> This text focuses on the staging and performance of Greek theatre. The author attempts to integrate classical and modern theatre, while providing a great deal of information about a number of the most important plays from the classical Greek period.

Wise, Jennifer, *Dionynsus Writes: The Invention of Theatre in Ancient Greece,* Cornell University Press, 1998.

The author discusses the relationship between literature and theatre by examining the influences of a newly emerging literary world on drama. This text also provides some interesting ideas about the role of the oral tradition on theatre.

Zelenak, Michael X., *Gender and Politics in Greek Tragedy,* Peter Lang, 1998.

This book offers some insight into the status of women in Greek culture and theatre and provides interesting analysis of many women characters from Greek drama.

Ingram Content Group UK Ltd.
Milton Keynes UK
UKHW010807190623
423681UK00015B/596